FARM ANIMALS

UNCOMMON
FARM ANIMALS

Ann Larkin Hansen
ABDO Publishing Company

visit us at
www.abdopub.com

Published by Abdo Publishing Company 4940 Viking Drive, Edina, Minnesota 55435.
Copyright © 1998 by Abdo Consulting Group, Inc. International copyrights reserved in
all countries. No part of this book may be reproduced in any form without written
permission from the publisher.

Printed in the United States.

Cover Photo credits: Peter Arnold, Inc.
Interior Photo credits: Peter Arnold, Inc.

Edited by Lori Kinstad Pupeza

Library of Congress Cataloging-in-Publication Data

Hansen, Ann Larkin.
        Uncommon farm animals / Ann Larkin Hansen.
        p. cm. -- (Farm animals)
        Includes index.
        Summary: Describes some of the more unusual animals that can be found on
        farms today, including ostriches, buffalo, and pygmy goats.
        ISBN 1-56239-607-2
        1. Domestic animals--Juvenile literature. [1. Domestic animals.] I. Title. II.
        Series: Hansen, Ann Larkin. Farm animals.
        SF75.5.H36   1998
        636--dc20   96-12464
                                                           CIP
                                                           AC

About the Author
Ann Larkin Hansen has a degree in history from the University of St. Thomas
in St. Paul, Minnesota. She currently lives with her husband and three boys
on a farm in northern Wisconsin, where they raise beef cattle, chickens, and
assorted other animals.

Contents

All Kinds of Animals

Not all cows are black and white, and not all pigs are pink. Not all farms raise ordinary farm animals. All around the country are farms that raise unusual, amusing, and rare animals.

There are **ostrich**, **mink**, and **trout** farms. There are farms dedicated to saving **rare breeds** of cows, pigs, and chickens. There are farms that raise wild animals, and animals from different parts of the world.

Opposite page: An American elk, largest member of the deer family.

Big Bird Farms

Ostriches have eyes the size of tennis balls, and their eggs are 24 times as big as a chicken's egg! They come from Africa, where they have been raised on farms for more than 100 years. Now there are ostrich farms in the United States, too.

The ostrich has cousins, like the **Rhea** from South America and the **Emu** from Australia. These birds are also being raised in this country. None of these birds can fly, but they are huge and fast. They are raised for meat, eggs, feathers, and leather.

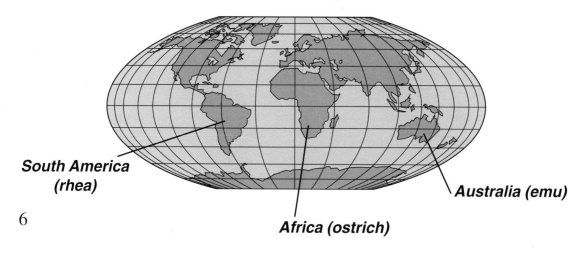

South America
(rhea)

Africa (ostrich)

Australia (emu)

Ostriches on an ostrich farm in South Africa.

Little Birds

All kinds of **fowl** are raised on farms. Ducks, turkeys, and geese have always been found on American farms. Now you can also find **pheasant**, **peacocks**, and **guinea fowl**!

These birds come from Asia, India, and Africa. They can be used for eggs, meat, and feathers. Geese also make good watchdogs, and guinea fowl eat a lot of bugs.

Most of these birds can be ordered from special catalogs. Many farmers raise a few unusual birds just for the fun of having them around.

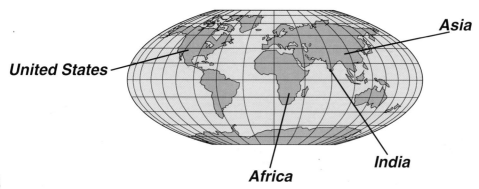

Muscovy ducks sitting on a fence in Decorah, Iowa.

Elk, Deer, and Buffalo

Some farmers have found they can make more money raising elk, deer, or buffalo instead of beef cattle. They must build fences six feet (1.8 m) high or more for these animals. Cattle only need fences three or four feet (about one meter) high.

Elk, deer, and buffalo are more wild than cattle. But they don't need as much grain, and they are often healthier. Buffalo, elk, and some deer are American. Other deer are from Europe and Australia and are called **fallow deer**.

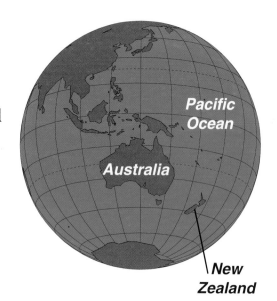

Pacific Ocean

Australia

New Zealand

A deer farm in New Zealand.

Wool, Work, and Friendship

In the mountains of South America, the Native Americans of Peru have raised **llamas** and **alpacas** for thousands of years. Llamas and alpacas stand about four feet (1.2 meters) high at the shoulder, and have long, skinny necks. They grow fine, long wool that is made into beautiful sweaters and other clothes.

Llamas and alpacas are also used to carry camping gear and other equipment. They are gentle and friendly. They are becoming popular in this country.

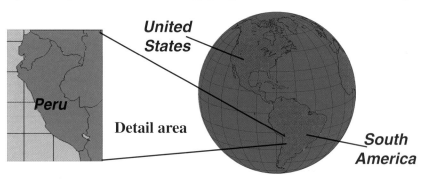

A young llama.

Miniatures

Some country people like small animals. Years of careful breeding have created miniature horses. These tiny animals are no bigger than big dogs. They pull tiny carts.

There are also **pygmy goats** and miniature sheep, called Babydoll Southdown sheep. **Donkeys** are not miniature, but they are very small, and good company. Donkeys, also called **burros**, can be used to guard flocks of sheep.

Opposite page: A miniature Shetland pony

Nibblers

Rabbits and **chinchillas** can be good pets in the city or on a farm. Chinchillas look like rabbits with short ears and long tails. They come from South America, and are raised for their wonderful fur.

Rabbits and chinchillas are kept in **hutches**, which are cages made of wood and wire. Four stout legs keep the cages off the ground. Rabbits and chinchillas eat special feed, and especially love fresh grass and clover. Instead of cows in a barn, some farmers keep rabbits in hutches.

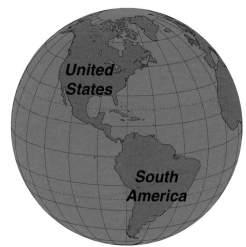

A chinchilla.

Bugs

Some bugs eat other bugs that harm plants. **Ladybug beetles**, **parasitic wasps**, and **praying mantises** are used by vegetable growers to control insect pests.

But bees are the bugs most often seen on farms. Their wooden **hives** are kept in a sunny corner where they aren't bothered by lots of traffic. Bees are important for two reasons: they make honey, and they **pollinate** plants. Plants cannot grow fruit if they are not pollinated.

Opposite page: A beekeeper working on a bee farm.

Disappearing Animals

A hundred years ago, there were a hundred or more different **breeds** of chicken. Now just two are raised by big poultry farms: **Leghorn chickens** for eggs, and **Rock-Cornish Cross chicken** for meat.

Instead of many different breeds of cows for milk, now we have mostly **Holstein cows**. The old breeds of farm animals are very rare. There were lots of breeds of sheep long ago, now there are few.

The breeds of farm animals used today are the best at producing the most food. But they are not the toughest, or the healthiest, or the prettiest. They are not usually very good at taking care of themselves.

**A rare breed of sheep, the Navajo Churro,
a four-horned ram.**

Preserving Rare Breeds

Today there are organizations for preserving old **breeds** of farm animals. These groups work with farmers across the country. Many breeds that had almost disappeared are now making a comeback. **Navajo Churro sheep** were almost wiped out in the 1950s, but there are now several flocks. **Fainting goats**, **Clydesdale horses**, **Dominique chickens** and **Tamworth hogs** are all slowly building in numbers. Keep your eyes open for a **Belted Galloway cow**—she looks like a walking Oreo cookie!

Opposite page: A herd of cattle in Australia.

Keeping Animals Alive

Keeping unusual animals is fun, but it is also a lot of work. They often need special feed that is hard to find. They may need special types of fencing or cages. The animals can be hard to find, and expensive to buy.

But many of these animals would be **extinct** if farmers had not taken care of them. Many farmers think it is important to preserve these animals, no matter how much work it takes.

Opposite page: A pair of emus.

All Sorts of Animals

There seems to be no end to all the sorts of animals that are kept on farms. Earthworms are used to make the soil healthy for crops, and also sold to fishermen for bait. **Pot-bellied pigs** from Vietnam and **Pygmy Hedgehogs** from Africa are kept just as pets. **Trout**, **shrimp**, and **crayfish** are raised for food. Game farms keep animals usually found only in the wilderness, like **mink** and fox. You can never be sure just what kind of animals you will find on a farm!

Opposite page: An earthworm.

Glossary

Alpaca—a type of llama with especially long, silky wool.

Belted Galloway Cattle—a breed of cattle that is black on the ends with a white belt around the middle, often called the "Oreo cookie cow."

Breeds—different types of the same animal, like different flavors of ice cream. For example, Beagles and Cocker Spaniels are breeds of dogs.

Burro—a small member of the horse family, domesticated about 5000 years ago. It has long ears, a tufted tail, and a loud bray.

Chinchilla—a rodent from South America that looks like a small rabbit with little ears and a long tail. It is raised for fur.

Clydesdale Horse—one of several draft (work) horse breeds that nearly became extinct when the tractor came into widespread use.

Crayfish—a small freshwater crustacean with little lobster-like claws.

Dominique Chicken—a tough, black and white barred chicken that is an ancestor to many of today's breeds.

Donkey—a burro.

Emu—a large flightless bird native to Australia, raised for meat. It is second only to the ostrich in size.

Extinct—no longer in existence.

Fainting Goats—a breed of goat that falls over when startled.

Fallow Deer—a small deer from Europe with a reddish-yellow coat that has white spots in summer.

Fowl—any large bird.

Guinea Fowl—a 20-inch (50 cm) tall bird with a bare neck native to Madagascar and sub-Saharan Africa.

Hive—a wooden box for sheltering bees and collecting their honey.

Holstein Cow—one of the largest cattle breeds, the Holstein dominates the dairy industry due to her enormous milk production.

Hutch—a cage on legs, usually built of wood and wire, for keeping rabbits or other small animals.

Ladybug Beetle—a small, rounded beetle with spotted back that feeds on many insect pests.

Leghorn Chicken—a white, high-strung chicken that lays more eggs in a year than any other breed.

Llama—a relative of the camel native to the Andes Mountains of South America, and used for wool and as a pack animal. Llamas stand about 4 feet (1.2 m) tall.

Mink—a small, meat-eating mammal native to North America and raised for its fur.

Navajo Churro Sheep—a sheep with two-textured wool and four horns developed by the Navajo Indians from Spanish stock.

Ostrich—the largest bird in the world, usually 4 to 5 feet (1.5 m) tall, native to Africa. It is raised for meat, leather, and feathers, and can be ridden. Ostriches cannot fly.

Parasitic Wasp—a type of wasp that lays its eggs on other insects. The young wasps then feed on their host.

Peacock—a large pheasant from the dry forests of India and Africa, with especially beautiful tail feathers and a loud voice.

Pheasant—a colorful bird about the size of a chicken. In this country "pheasant" usually refers to the Chinese Ringneck variety. There are 175 species native to Asia, India, and Africa.

Pollinate—to transfer pollen from the stamen of one flower to the pistil of another, causing a fruit to form.

Pot-Bellied Pig—a small pig from Vietnam with a huge belly.

Praying Mantis—a long, slender insect that grabs other bugs in its forelegs and eats them.

Pygmy Goats—from Africa, these goats are about one-third the size of other goats but are good milkers.

Pygmy Hedgehog—a small, quilled rodent from Africa.

Rare Breeds—animals in danger of extinction.

Rhea—the "pampas ostrich," it is a large, flightless bird native to South America and raised for meat.

Rock-Cornish Cross chicken—a breed of chicken that grows especially fast and heavy.

Shrimp—a small crustacean that usually lives in the ocean and is highly prized as food.

Tamworth Hog—a reddish hog that is sunburn resistant and one of the oldest breeds known.

Trout—a type of fish usually found in cold, clear water.

Internet Sites

The Virtual Farm
http://www.manawatu.gen.nz/~tiros/ftour1.htm
A very impressive display including photos and sound. This site is all about dairy farming in New Zealand.

Virtual Pig Dissection
http://mail.fkchs.sad27.k12.me.us/fkchs/vpig/
Learn how to dissect a pig without hurting a pig. This is a really cool site that gets a lot of traffic.

Castalia Llamas
http://www.rockisland.com/~castalia/cllama.html
Chosen as a hotsite, featured on TV, listed in Popular Science's WebWatch. Full of llama facts, images and stories to amuse and bewilder. This is a cool site, check it out.

Museums in the Classroom
http://www.museum.state.il.us/mic_home/newton/project/
Prairie chickens and the prairie in Illinois by Mrs. Vanderhoof's third grade class and Mrs. Volk's fourth grade science classes.

These sites are subject to change. Go to your favorite search engine and type in "farm animals" for more sites.

PASS IT ON
Tell Others What You Like About Animals!

To educate readers around the country, pass on interesting tips about animals, maybe a fun story about your animal or pet, and little-known facts about animals. We want to hear from you!

To get posted on ABDO Publishings website, E-mail us at "animals@abdopub.com"

Index